PRESSURE WASHING 01 ESSENTIALS
Guide to a Successful Pressure Washing Business

AMEH EHI JAMES

2022

i

Dedication

This piece of work is dedicated to God Almighty.

Acknowledgement

My utmost and sincere gratitude goes to my Mum and Dad for all their sacrifice in training me, I pray God to give them long life and prosperity.

My profound gratitude goes to all the authors whose books I consulted in the process writing. Also, I wish to thank all my friends in the pressure washing business, especially; Walter T.J. (Jet Power), Jason (Jspray Pressure Washing and Services LLC & Charles Reynolds (Reynolds Pressure Washing LLC) for their motivations.

Also, I thank Mrs. Phyllis Griggs (profound children author and writer) for her inspiration and impacts in my life.

TABLE OF CONTENTS

INTRODUCTION

There is something so satisfying about pressure washing business that makes many people wanting to venture into it. But if there is anything more enjoyable, it is earning a 6-to-7-digit income through the business.

With low start-up costs and high-profit margins, starting a pressure washing business can be a perfect fit for many people seeking to start a business that can generate desired income. However, just like any other business, there is a lot you need to consider before starting. Such include; investments, insurance, strategies, and more.

To get you started on the right track and build a stable income flow with pressure washing business, this book was compiled with a step-by-step guide on how to start a pressure washing business and stable income.

There is market for pressure washing, no matter where you live. You can target homeowners, commercial establishments, or specialize in cleaning building exterior or driveways, decks, and patios. Offering window and chimney cleaning services is another option. To thrive in the pressure washing business, you must develop a good relationship with your clients.

MEANING OF PRESSURE WASHING

Pressure washing or power washing is the use of high-pressure water spray to remove loose paint, mold, grime, dust, mud, and dirt from surfaces and objects such as buildings, vehicles, path ways and concrete surfaces among others.

The terms pressure washing and power washing are used interchangeably in many scenarios, and there is some debate as to whether they are actually different processes. A pressure washing surface cleaner is a tool consisting of two to four high-pressure jets on a rotating bar that swivels when water is flowing. This action creates a uniformed cleaning pattern that can clean flat surfaces at a rapid rate.

Hydro-jet cleaning is a more powerful form of power washing, employed to remove buildup and debris in tanks and lines.

AREAS OF USE

Pressure washing is employed by businesses and home owners to reduce allergies, minimize hazards, and improve aesthetics. A pressure washer is used to clean surfaces such as:

- Gutters
- Roofs
- Decks
- Sidewalks
- Patios
- Driveways
- Siding
- Parking lots
- Cladding

Note: 1

Depending upon the surface to be cleaned, higher or lower pressure should be used, as well as the appropriate nozzle.

PRESSURE WASHING EQUIPMENT

Before you even get started, it is advisable to know the various equipment needed for a pressure washing business. Below are some pressure washing equipment;

Truck, van, & trailer: not only will you need to get around, but also your workbench, office & garage, so an appropriate vehicle(s) is required. An open or closed van and depending on your budget, purchase or rent one, there are pros and cons to both. You can also truck wrap the closed truck and use it as an affordable & effective marketing tactic. However, a truck alone isn't enough and you'll need a trailer or even a pressure washer.

Nozzles: High pressure washer nozzles blast away dirt effortlessly and quickly with a jackhammer effect. Turbo nozzles are great for caked-on mud and build-up on construction equipment.

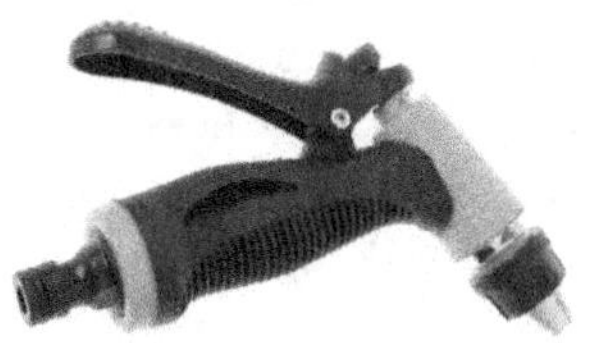

Surface cleaners: Designed for use with most hot and cold water pressure washers, flat surface cleaners are ideal for cleaning floors, parking lots, warehouse floors, trailer floors, and more.

Water Recovery System: Recover wash water and help the environment while staying compliant. Wash water recovery is required by many cities and states. The RC Series can make a complicated wash water recovery simple. With a compact footprint and a drain port at the bottom of the tank provides an easy option to clean out sludge recovered.

Dual Lance: This 36-inch-long lance is designed for hot water use and can be used with water temperatures up to 220 degrees. Hotsy quality through and through. Superior heat protection with zytel insulated grip and a side handle.

Wands: 6- to 24-foot extension wands are ideal for high or hard-to-reach cleaning areas. They can be used with any pressure washers up to 4000 PSI. Whereas, on a low reach, short pressure washing wand can be used.

Pressure Washer Soap & Detergents: The right kinds of pressure washer detergent, soaps and cleaning supplies can make your equipment last longer. Hotsy Continuous Clean (HCC) additives in their power washer soaps are specially formulated to stop equipment corrosion and prevent soap and hard water build-up.

Water Hose Reels: You need them for storing and organizing your hoses.

EASY STEPS TO START A PRESSURE WASHING BUSINESS

Starting a pressure washing business is approachable and lucrative. You will be ready to start after taking some advice from other industry experts and following these steps to turn your business into a profitable venture.

i. **Strategizing Your Business**

Power and pressure washing seems pretty straightforward, but if you have done your research into the industry and the direction it's going in, you will see that there are a few things you need to iron out before hitting the streets.

If you're a power washing beginner then you should look into learning about this service before offering it to clients. You could seriously damage someone's property if you use your equipment incorrectly.

-**Know Your Service Offerings**

The very first thing you need to do is decide on what your core service offerings are and who you'll be servicing (i.e. residential, commercial, or industrial). Be focused. Don't take on too much too quickly. Some projects might be bigger and more intense than what you and your equipment can handle.

- **Know your scope**

The second thing you will have to iron out is your service offering scope. Some service providers focus on specific jobs, such as restoration, paint removal, general maintenance, windows, roofs and gutters, concrete, interlock, and more. Some service providers also offer window washing and other home cleaning services.

You don't have to do it all, you just have to do what you're good at and focus on it. Once you're a pro you'll be able to take on bigger clients and bigger contracts.

For example, it took Kris Cook, Owner of KC Power Clean, thirteen years to grow his business into the fully fledged power washing company that it is today. By then, he was approached by Starbucks to do some paint removal work. This, in turn, led to an opportunity to provide the accompanying sandblasting service. This pivot helped him grow his business after buying the appropriate equipment and employee hands to help him do that.

ii. **Get Your Power Washing Equipment**

Your equipment needs will vary based on your service offering and scope. For example, if you're just focused on pressure washing for residential clients, then you'll need a pressure washer with a force of 3,500 PSI and above, hoses, first and second story reach nozzles, and a downstream valve. If you're going to be doing commercial work, then you'll need stronger equipment with more functionalities and your own water reservoir.

Note 2:

"As far as equipment goes, we're in an industry that isn't super technologically advanced, but there are some pieces of equipment out there, like the water-fed pole, or pure water cleaning in general, that are faster and safer".

Jersey, WCR Nation

iii.   **Create Your Brand**

Creating your company brand doesn't have to be time-consuming and expensive. Focus on the following necessities.

-   **Company Name and Logo**

You need a business name and logo if you're ready to start taking on jobs. You'll also need these things to register your business.

Put your name and phone on your company vehicles (using decals), uniforms, quotes, emails, invoices, and marketing and advertising materials. For instance;

For professional brand logo and other designs, you can reach out to 'Xtreme Publishing Media' via face page to get yours done.

- **Contact information**

You can't run a business without an email, phone number, and website. Even if you're running a small operation it's a good idea to have a separate business phone number and email. This is especially helpful once your business starts growing. It's easier to keep track of your clients if they are separate from your personal life.

- **Grow your business with quote**

Quote helps your clients to know how much you charge for your job.

iv. **Marketing on Social**

Setting up a social media account is one of the most important things to do when starting a pressure washing business. It can be very overwhelming though: you need to post regularly, at the right times, and engage with your community to get good liftoff. We recommend getting on at least one social network. If you can mange two, even better.

Facebook is likely your best bet for the pressure washing industry due to its broad user base and extensive reach. Many

Facebook users are likely to own houses or commercial establishments, making it an excellent place to advertise your pressure washing services.

Post pictures of your services, customer testimonials, and offers to boost engagement and gain exposure for your company. You can also ask your existing customers to share your post or post reviews to generate word-of-mouth publicity.

You can also distribute flyers, use vehicle wraps, or opt for the classic door-to-door advertising tactic. You never know what may work and get you your next client!

This is a professional flyer for Jspray Pressure Washing and Services LLC. You can get yours done by contacting 'Xtreme Publishing Media' on facebook.

- What social profile should look like

Profiles on social media networks will include different information sections. For example, a Facebook Business page will include an entire "about" page, whereas Instagram will give you only 150 characters to tell people about your account.

The most important things to include in any social profile are your business name, business information, website link, and contact in the account profile. You can also include a work request link right on your profile in the link in your bio, or directly in your profile on some social networks, such as Facebook.

Use these social networks to post content about your services and other helpful power washing information.

- What you should Post

The type of content you post on social is entirely up to you. The most effective social media content is typically more helpful than it is promotional. Professional social media marketers go by the 80/20 rule. This means that only 20 percent of your content should be promotional (i.e. deals, promotions, and services offered), and the other 80 percent should be other types of content (i.e. when you should hire a professional, home care maintenance best practices, or those satisfying power washing videos everyone loves).

v. **Insure and Register your Business**

Power and pressure washing business owners have quite a bit of liability on their hands. Your equipment can cause a lot of damage if used incorrectly or if you make a mistake. It's wise to invest in general liability insurance to help protect and separate you from your business's liability.

You should also register your business with your local government. Do some research and figure out what steps you need to take to register your business.

Establishing your business as an LLC will go a long way in separating your personal assets from your business assets. Depending on where you live, you may need to pay a bond, get a business permit, register your business for sales tax, and get an environmental permit.

vi. **Plan Ahead**

Start thinking about your business long term right now. How you can start growing in six months, twelve months, and two years from now? This might seem like you're jumping the gun, but you're not. If you have any desire to grow your business in any capacity, then you need to start thinking the next step ahead. In planning ahead, here are some tips;

- **Price your services for profit.** Don't rely on the competition. Use a proper formula to come up with your pressure washing price list.
- **Make appointment bookings easy.** After your client pays an invoice, send them a thank-you email along with an opportunity to schedule the next job.
- **Automate your client emails.** Create some email templates that you can send to your clients when you give them quotes, invoices, and accept payments so

you can stay in touch every step of the way.

- **Improve client retention with special offers.** Offer discounted rates for follow-up appointments.
- **Offer referral discounts.** Give clients who refer you to their friends and family free services or discounts so they can network for you.

GUIDE FOR A SUCCESSFUL PRESSURE WASHING BUSINESS PLAN

Are you about starting a pressure washing or power washing business? if yes, here is a complete sample pressure washing business plan template & free feasibility study. One of the very businesses that you may want to consider starting is the pressure washing business. This business is sure a unique one and the point is that every day more and more people have continued to smile to the bank. If you are looking for a very profitable business to commence, then you need to look in the direction of the pressure washing business. Below is a business plan sample that will guide you on starting a profitable one;

Industry Overview

Pressure washing businesses make use of pressure washers to carry out their washing services and a pressure washer or power washer as it is also called is basically a high-pressure mechanical sprayer that is used to remove stuffs such as clogged oil, greasy stains, unwanted graffiti, loose paint, mold, grime, dust, mud, and dirt from surfaces and objects like building facilities, bridges, ships, vehicles and concrete surfaces.

Usually, high-pressure water mixed with special cleaning chemicals, aids in the removal of stubborn stains such as greasy stains, clogged oil, graffiti, and loose paints et al especially when the water is hot, as a quick rinse of the softened graffiti.

No doubt, the Pressure Washing industry is in the mature stage of its life cycle. Over the last 10 years, the industry is projected to improve its contribution to the United States' economy by 3.6 percent.

The Pressure Washing industry is expected to grow a little faster than the overall economy; this is due to a steep revenue declines and profit margin contractions at the start of the stated period, effectively skewing IVA growth rates. Going forward, in the next five years, the Pressure Washing industry IVA and GDP are expected to increase at a steady rate.

Just like any other business, the demand for pressure washing services usually declined during recession period / economic downturn and this is due to the declining household spending on cleaning services and reduced demand from business clients. As the economy grow, and income increases, there will be corresponding increase in the demand for cleaning related services such as pressure washing services.

The Pressure Washing industry is indeed a very large industry and pretty much thriving in all the parts of the world especially in developed countries such as United States of America, Canada, United Kingdom, Germany, Australia and Italy et al.

As a matter of fact, there are no companies with a leading market share in the industry. Statistics has it that in the united states of America alone, there are about 135,302 licensed and registered pressure washing businesses responsible for employing about 187,073 employees and the industry rakes in a whooping sum of $9bn annually with an annual growth rate projected at 0.5 percent

Based on the industry overview above, it is no doubt that the pressure washing industry is gaining high patronage from clients every day.

Executive Summary

The name of our company is Prime Pressure® Washing Company. We are a standard pressure washing business that is incorporated under the law of the United States of America. Our head office will be located in a densely populated business district in the heart of Atlanta-Georgia, U.S.

We are strategically positioned in between a residential center and an industrial hub and we are set to services the whole of the community both corporate clients and individual clients alike.

Our basic service offering to our highly esteemed customers as a pressure washing company will revolve around Swimming pool cleaning & maintenance, Parking lot sweeping, Drain & gutter cleaning, Graffiti removal /

washing, Snowplowing, Ventilation duct cleaning, Chimney sweep services, Window washing, Drain, duct and gutter cleaning, Pool maintenance, Parking lot and driveway washing, Chimney sweep services, Providing other outdoor maintenance services and other cleaning services.

Although our intention of starting a pressure washing business is to offer only the above stated services, but we will not close our doors to diversification (additional services) as long as it does not affect our core services. In the bid to maximize our position as the leading pressure washing company in Atlanta – Georgia.

Prime Pressure® Washing Company is located in a full-serviced state of the art pressure washing cum cleaning facility which has the following features: a seventy foot fully automatic tunnel; 3 high pressure wand self-service bays; and 5 vacuum stations complete with fragrance and carpet shampoo dispensing machines, Insulator washers with a pump pressure of about 1000 psi and a nozzle pressure between 500 and

750 psi, centrifugal water pump, stainless steel water storage tank, high-pressure water hose, high-pressure dead-man type water wash gun and Electrical grounds for the wash gun and washing system

We will offer both in-station and out-off station services. Our customers will have the options of choosing from our different packages – we have the plans to serve both individual clients (households) and corporate clients (industries and the government) as well which is why we designed various packages.

At Prime Pressure® Washing Company we are passionate in the pursuit of excellence and financial success with uncompromising services and integrity which is why we have decided to start our own pressure cleaning business; we are in the industry to make a positive mark.

We are quite optimistic that our values and quality of service offering will help us drive our pressure washing business to enviable heights and also help us attract the numbers of clients that will make the business highly profitable. We are a company that will be dedicated to establishing good business relationship with our clients giving them value for their money and reasons for them to hire our services over and over again.

We are quite aware that in order to become the number one choice in our city, we must continue to deliver quality pressure washing services and that is exactly what we will do. We are open to the use of latest technology in the pressure washing industry. No doubt our excellent customer service and the range of services we offer will position us to always welcome repeated customers.

Prime Pressure® Washing Company is owned and managed by Mr. Piers Reagan and Family. Piers Reagan has well over 15 years of experience managing some of the leading pressure washing companies and industrial cleaning brands in different cities in the United States of America and Canada prior to starting Prime Pressure® Washing Company.

Our Products and Services

Prime Pressure® Washing Company is a standard and well-equipped pressure washing company that offer a wide range of services that revolves around the pressure washing cum industrial cleaning industry and other complementary services.

We intend giving our customers every reason to always come back which is why we have customized our services. Basically, our services will involve us going out to services of clients' needs. These are the services we will offer as a pressure washing company;

- Swimming pool cleaning & maintenance
- Parking lot sweeping
- Graffiti removal / washing
- Drain & gutter cleaning
- Snowplowing
- Ventilation duct cleaning
- Chimney sweep services
- Window washing
- Drain, duct and gutter cleaning
- Pool maintenance

- Parking lot and driveway washing
- Chimney sweep services
- Providing other outdoor maintenance services
- Other related industrial cleaning services

Our Mission and Vision Statement

- Our Vision is to become the number one pressure washing company in the whole of Atlanta – Georgia with active presence in major cities in the United States of America and Canada.
- Our mission as a pressure washing company is to develop a highly successful, profitable all round pressure washing business which provides quality services in our community and to become a standard for an ideal pressure washing business not only in the State of Georgia but also throughout the United States of America and Canada where we intend selling our franchise.

Our Business Structure

We are quite aware that the success of any business lies in the foundation on which the business is built on, which is why we have decided to build our pressure washing company on the right business foundation.

As a matter of fact, we are set out to build a pressure washing business that will be a standard for the pressure washing cum industrial cleaning industry in the United States of America and Canada. We want to build a business of dedicated workforce who will go all the way to ensure that our customers are satisfied and they get value for their money.

In other to achieve this, we are aware that it takes a business with the right employees and structure to achieve all what we have set to achieve, which is why will be putting structures and processes in place that will help us deliver excellent services and run the business on auto pilot. The success of our pressure washing business will be anchored on the team not on any individual.

With the wide range of our service offerings, we are only expected to employ more than it is required to run a conventional pressure washing business. Definitely, we will have various employees to man the various services offering of Prime Pressure® Washing Company.

Prime Pressure® Washing Company will employ professionals and skilled people to occupy the following position;

- Manager (Owner)
- Accountant/Cashier
- Marketing and Sales Executive
- Client Service Executive
- Cleaners/Pressure Machine Operators (6)
- Truck/Van` Driver

Tips: If you are running a self-operated pressure washing business, you may not be needing all these staff.

Job Roles and Responsibilities

There are several roles that needs to be occupied in the pressure washing business; here they are;

Manager (Owner):
-   Responsible for providing direction for the business
-   Creating, communicating, and implementing the organization's vision, mission, and overall direction i.e. leading the development and implementation of the overall organization's strategy.
-   Responsible for fixing prices and signing business deals and payment of salaries.
-   Responsible for signing checks and documents on behalf of the company.
-   Evaluates the success of the organization
-   Responsible for managing the daily activities in the organization.
-   Ensure that the facility is in tip top shape and conducive enough to welcome customers etc.

Marketing and Sales Executive

- Identifies, prioritizes, and reaches out to new clients, and business opportunities et al.
- Identifies development opportunities; follows up on development leads and contacts; participates in the structuring and financing of projects; assures the completion of projects.
- Writes winning proposal documents, negotiate fees and rates in line with organizations' policy.
- Responsible for handling business research, market surveys and feasibility studies for clients.
- Responsible for supervising implementation, advocate for the customer's needs, and communicate with clients etc.

Accountant/Cashier

- Responsible for preparing financial reports, budgets, and financial statements for the organization.
- Provides managements with financial analyses, development budgets, and accounting reports; analyzes financial feasibility for the most complex proposed

projects; conducts market research to forecast trends and business conditions.

- Responsible for financial forecasting and risks analysis.
- Performs cash management, general ledger accounting, and financial reporting for the organization etc.

Client Service Executive

- Welcomes clients and visitors by greeting them in person or on the telephone; answering or directing inquiries.
- Ensures that all contacts with clients (e-mail, walk-In center, SMS or phone) provides the client with a personalized customer service experience of the highest level.
- Through interaction with clients on the phone, uses every opportunity to build client's interest in the company's products and services etc.

Cleaners/Pressure machine Operators

- Responsible for handling core services that revolve around Swimming pool cleaning & maintenance, Parking lot sweeping, Drain & gutter cleaning, Graffiti removal/washing, Snowplowing, Ventilation duct cleaning,

Chimney sweep services, Window washing, Drain, duct and gutter cleaning, Pool maintenance, Parking lot and driveway washing, Chimney sweep services, Providing other outdoor maintenance services and other industrial cleaning services et al as requested by clients.

- Clean up after customers and clean work area.
- Maintain a clean working area by sweeping, vacuuming, dusting, cleaning of glass doors and windows, etc. if required.

Truck/Van Driver:

- Responsible for transporting equipment, supplies and workers to project site.
- Delivers completed cleaning jobs that care movable to clients as requested.
- Runs errand for the organization.
- Handles any other duty as assigned by the manager etc.

SWOT Analysis

Pressure washing business is one of the many businesses that can easily generate sales with little stress, as long as it is well positioned and equipped to carry out the various services. We are building a standard pressure washing business with variety of services which is why we have decided to subject our business idea (company) to SWOT Analysis.

Ordinarily we can successfully run a normal pressure washing business without the stress of going through the required protocol of setting up a new business including writing a detailed business plan, but because of the nature of the kind of pressure washing business we want to establish, we don't have any option other than to follow due process.

We hired the services of Mr. Coleman Carrington, an HR and Business consultant with bias in startups to help us conduct SWOT analysis for our company and he did a pretty job for us. Here is a of the result we got from the SWOT analysis that was conducted on behalf of Prime Pressure® Washing Company Atlanta-Georgia;

- **Strength:**

Prime Pressure® Washing Company is centrally located in a densely populated industrial and residential estate in Atlanta-Georgia; our location is in fact one of our major strength. We have a well equipped state of the art facility and we are also one of the very few pressure washing companies in the whole of Atlanta-Georgia that offers a wide range of services for both households and industries.

Another strength that counts for us is the power of our team; our workforce and management. We have a team that are considered experts in the pressure washing cum industrial cleaning industry, a team of hardworking and dedicated individuals.

- **Weakness:**

Prime Pressure® Washing Company is a new business which is owned by an individual (family), and we may not have the financial muscle to sustain the kind of publicity we want to give our business and also to attract some of the technocrats in the pressure washing and industrial cleaning industry.

- **Opportunities:**

We are centrally located in one of the busiest areas in Atlanta-Georgia and are open to all the available opportunities that the city has to offer. Our business concept also positions us to be a one stop shop in the pressure washing and industrial cleaning industry. The truth is that there are no standard and well-equipped pressure washing businesses within the area where ours is going to be located; the closest industrial cleaning facility to our proposed location is about 6 miles away. In a nutshell, we do not have any direct competition within our target market area.

- **Threat:**

Some of the threats that are likely going to confront Prime Pressure® Washing Company is unfavorable government policies, seasonal fluctuations, demographic/social factors, downturn in the economy which is likely going to affect consumers spending and of course emergence of new competitors within the same location where ours is located.

Market Analysis

- **Market Trends**

The pressure washing and industrial cleaning market is a market that is dependent on loads of factors. The fact that it helps keep our environment clean and also help in saving energy gives room for people to patronize the business. As a matter of fact, it is now common and trendy to find pressure washing and industrial cleaning companies leveraging on 'Climate Change and Save Energy' to market their services.

Of course, pressure washing and industrial cleaning business responds to the increase in household spending and improvement in the economy; which is why it has become trendy to find pressure washing and industrial cleaning businesses located around areas where residence and businesses can show that they can afford the services.

Another common trend in the pressure washing and industrial cleaning industry is that in the bid to survive global economic melt down and to ensure steady flow of income to effectively run the business, most pressure washing and industrial cleaning companies engage in other related services. Some of them even go as far as establishing a car wash, snow removal services and a carpet cleaning business simply because they all fall within same line of business.

- **Our Target Market**

Before choosing a location for our pressure washing and industrial cleaning business, we conducted our feasibility studies and market survey and we were able to identify those who will benefit greatly from our service offerings. Basically, those who will benefit from our service offering are households, facility managers, industries (manufacturing plants) and government et al. They cut across various different sectors of the economy.

The demographic component of those who need the services of a pressure washing and industrial cleaning services spreads across the public sector, the organized private sector, and individuals from different strata of the society and from all walks of life but most importantly every one need to clean up the exterior of the buildings and drainages et al no matter their income level.

Residential and public places needs it more often than the others though. Below is a list of the people and organizations which our pressure washing and industrial cleaning services is designed for;

- The public sector; government ministries, agencies and parastatals.
- Organized private sector
- Households
- Facility managers
- Restaurants
- Hotels and Motels
- Residential areas
- Religious Centers
- Warehouses
- Retail locations
- Educational Facilities
- Lounges

Casinos
- Medical facility
- Bars.

Our competitive advantage

Pressure washing and industrial cleaning business is an easy to set up business that does not require formal training to achieve; anybody can set a pressure washing and industrial cleaning business if they have the required startup capital and informal training on how to operate the various presser washers.

It means that the possibility of pressure washing and industrial cleaning businesses springing up in the location where ours is located can't be ruled out. We aware of this, which is why we decided to come up with a business concept that will position us to become the leader in Atlanta -Georgia.

Our competitive edge is that we are a standard business and well-equipped pressure washing and industrial cleaning business that has loads of complimentary business offerings that can easily assist us in attracting both corporate and individual customers within the radius of our business operations.

We can confidently say that the location of our pressure washing and industry cleaning business will definitely count as a positive for us amongst any competitor that might start a pressure washing business or any other related cleaning business in same location where ours is located.

For the time being, Prime Pressure® Washing Company has no real competitors that can compete with the quality of services we offer and our business offerings et al. Our customer service will be customized to meet the needs of all our customers.

Lastly, all our employees will be well taken care of, and their welfare package will be among the best within our category (startups pressure washing business and other related industrial cleaning businesses in the United States) in the industry. It will enable them to be more than willing to build the business with us and help deliver our set goals and achieve all our business aims and objectives.

Sales and marketing Strategy

- **Sources of Income**

Prime Pressure® Washing Company is established with the aim of maximizing profits in the pressure washing and industrial cleaning industry and we are going to go all the way out to ensure that we do all it takes to attract both individual clients and corporate clients on a regular basis.

Prime Pressure® Washing Company will generate income by offering the following services;

- Swimming pool cleaning & maintenance
- Parking lot sweeping

- Graffiti removal / washing
- Drain & gutter cleaning
- Snowplowing
- Ventilation duct cleaning
- Chimney sweep services
- Window washing
- Drain, duct and gutter cleaning
- Pool maintenance
- Parking lot and driveway washing
- Chimney sweep services
-Providing other outdoor maintenance services
- Other related industrial cleaning services.

Sales Forecast

One thing is certain; there would always be corporate organization and individual clients who would need the services of pressure washing and industrial cleaning business.

We are well positioned to take on the available market in Atlanta – Georgia and we are quite optimistic that we will meet our set target of generating enough income/profits from the first six month of operations and grow our pressure washing and industrial cleaning business and our clientele base.

We have been able to critically examine the pressure washing and industrial cleaning industry – market and we have analyzed our chances in the industry and we have been able to come up with the following sales forecast. The sales projection are based on information gathered on the field and some assumptions that are peculiar to similar startups in Atlanta – Georgia.

Below is the sales projection for Prime Pressure® Washing Company, it is based on the location of our business and of course the wide range of related services that we will be offering;

- **First Year-:** $200,000
- **Second Year-:** $450,000
- **Third Year-:** $750,000

N.B: This projection is done based on what is obtainable in the pressure washing and industrial cleaning industry and with the assumption that there won't be any major economic meltdown and there won't be any major competitor offering same additional dance related services as we do within same location. Please note that the above projection might be lower and at the same time it might be higher.

- **Marketing Strategy and Sales Strategy**

The marketing strategy for Prime Pressure® Washing Company is going to be driven basically by excellent customers service and quality service delivery. We will ensure that we build a loyal customer base. We want to drive sales via the output of our jobs and via referral from our satisfied customers.

We are quite aware of how satisfied customers drive business growth especially businesses like pressure washing and industrial cleaning and related services.

Prime Pressure® Washing Company is a pressure washing and industrial cleaning business that is strategically located and we are going to maximize the opportunities that is available which is why we spend more to locate the business in a location that will be visible and accessible to our target market.

Prime Pressure® Washing Company is set to make use of the following marketing and sales strategies to attract clients;

- Introduce our carpet cleaning business by sending introductory letters alongside our brochure to corporate organizations, households and key stake holders in Page – Arizona.

- Print out fliers and business cards and strategically drop them in offices, libraries, public facilities and train stations et al.
- Use friends and family to spread word about our business
- Post information about our carpet cleaning company and the services we offer on bulletin boards in places like schools, libraries, and local coffee shops et al.
- Placing a small or classified advertisement in the newspaper, or local publication about our carpet cleaning company and the services we offer.
- Leverage on referral networks such as agencies that will attract clients who would need our customized services.

Publicity and Advertising Strategy

Prime Pressure® Washing Company is set to create a standard for pressure washing and industrial cleaning business in Atlanta – Georgia and throughout the United States which is why we will go all the way to adopt and apply best practices to promote our business.

Good enough there is no hard and fast rule on how to advertise or promote a pressure washing and industrial cleaning business. The challenge is that most pressure washing and industrial cleaning companies do not have the required money to pump into publicity and advertising. The cash they have will be reserved to take care of overhead and operational cost.

We will ensure that we leverage on all conventional and non – conventional publicity and advertising technique to promote our pressure washing and industrial cleaning business. Here are the platforms we intend leveraging on to promote and advertise Prime Pressure® Washing Company;

- Encourage our loyal customers to help us use Word of Mouth mode of advertisement (referrals).
- Advertise our pressure washing and industrial cleaning business in relevant magazines, local newspaper, local TV stations and local radio station.
- Promote our business online via our official website
- List our business on local directories (yellow pages).
- Sponsor relevant community programs.

Our Pricing Strategy

Our pricing system is going to be based on what is obtainable in the pressure washing and industrial cleaning industry, we don't intend to charge more (except for premium and customized services) and we don't intend to charge less than our competitors are offering in Atlanta – Georgia.

Be that as it may, we have put plans in place to offer discount services once in a while and also to reward our loyal customers especially when they refer clients to us. The prices of our services will be same as what is obtainable in the open market.

- **Payment Options**

At Prime Pressure® Washing Company, our payment policy will be all inclusive because we are quite aware that different clients would prefer different payment options as it suits them. Here are the payment options that we will make available to our clients;

-Payment by via bank transfer

-Payment via online bank transfer

-Payment via check

-Payment via bank draft

-Payment via mobile money

-Payment with cash

In view of the above, we have chosen banking platforms that will help us achieve our plans with little or no itches.

Startup Expenditure (Budget)

We have been able to pull cash that will be enough for us to successfully launch a standard pressure washing and industrial cleaning company in Atlanta – Georgia, US.

These are the key areas where we will spend our start-up capital on;

- The Total Fee for Registering the Business in Atlanta – Georgia – $750.

- Legal expenses for obtaining licenses and permits – $1,500.
- Marketing promotion expenses (2,000 flyers at $0.04 per copy) for the total amount of $3,580.
- Cost for hiring Business Consultant – $2,000.
- Insurance (general liability, workers' compensation and property casualty) coverage at a total premium – $30,800.
- Cost of accounting software, CRM software and Payroll Software – $3,000.
- Cost for leasing facility for the car wash – $70,000.
- Cost for facility remodeling – $50,000.
- Other start-up expenses including stationery – $1000).
- Phone and utility deposits – ($3,500).
- Operational cost for the first 3 months (salaries of employees, payments of bills et al) – $40,000.

- The cost for Start-up inventory – $15,000.
- Cost for store equipment (cash register, security, ventilation, signage) – $13,750.
- Cost of pressure washing and industrial cleaning equipment (a seventy foot fully automatic tunnel; 3 high pressure wand self-service bays; and 5 vacuum stations complete with fragrance and carpet shampoo dispensing machines, Insulator washers with a pump pressure of about 1000 psi and a nozzle pressure between 500 and 750 psi, centrifugal water pump, stainless steel water storage tank, high-pressure water hose, high-pressure dead-man type water wash gun and Electrical grounds for the wash gun and

washing system and Flexible pipes for water delivery et al)- $250,000.

- The cost for the purchase of furniture and gadgets (Computers, Printers, Telephone, TVs, tables and chairs et al): $4,000.
- The cost of Launching a Website: $600.
- The cost for our grand opening party: $1,500.
- Miscellaneous: $10,000.

We would need an estimate of $750,000 to successfully launch our pressure washing and industrial cleaning business in Atlanta – Georgia, US.

Generating Funding / Startup Prime Pressure® Washing Company

Prime Pressure® Washing Company is a business that will be owned and managed by Piers Reagan and Family. They are the sole financial of the business which is why they decided to restrict the sourcing of the start – up capital for the business to just three major sources.

These are the areas we intend generating our start – up capital;

- Generate part of the start – up capital from personal savings and sale of his stocks.
- Generate part of the start – up capital from friends and other extended family members
- Generate a larger chunk of the startup capital from the bank (loan facility).

N.B: We have been able to generate about $250,000 (Personal savings $200,000 and soft loan from family members $50,000) and we are at the final stages of obtaining a loan facility of $500,000 from our bank. All the papers and document has been duly signed and submitted, the loan has been approved and any moment from now our account will be credited.

Sustainability and Expansion Strategy

Part of the plans we have in place to sustain Prime Pressure® Washing Company is to ensure that we continue to deliver quality services, improvise on how to do things faster and cheaper. We are not going to relent in providing conducive environment for our workers and also the required trainings that will help them deliver excellent services at all times.

Template for a Successful Pressure Washing Quote

Your Company Name

Company Website

Your Phone Number
Your Email Address
Your Company Address
Your City, State, ZIP

Recipient

Client Company Name
Street Address
City, State, ZIP

Quote Subject
Quote Subject

Quote

Quote Number

Quote Sent:
Date Due

Service/Product	Description	Qty	Unit Cost	Total
				$ 0.00
				$ 0.00
				$ 0.00
				$ 0.00
				$ 0.00
				$ 0.00
				$ 0.00
				$ 0.00
				$ 0.00
				$ 0.00

Notes

Subtotal	$ 0.00	
Tax Rate & Total	5.00%	$ 0.00
Quote Total	**$ 0.00**	

CONCLUSION

The analysis in this book shows that pressure washing business is a profitable venture, if only the owner follows the right mechanisms. Pressure washing business is capable of thriving anywhere, depending on the management.

REFERENCES

Dave Lavinsky (2022). Pressure Washing Business Plan Template: Growthink, Ideas, Capitals, Action. Retrieved from growthink.com/business/plan/help-center/pressure-washing-plan,

Jobber (2022). Free Estimate Template. Retrieved from https://getjobbers.com.

KC Power Clean (2022). How to Start a Pressure Washing Business Scratch. Retrieved from academy.getjobber.com/resources/articles/how-to-start-ressur-washing-business.

OGS Capital (2018). Pressure Washing Business Plan Sample. Retrieved from ogscapital.com/article/pressure-washing-business-plan.

Profitable Venture Magazine Ltd (2022). How to Write a Pressure Washing Business Plan (Sample Template). Retrieved from profitableventure.com/pressure-washing-business-plan.

The Daily Egg (2002). 5 Easy Steps to Start a PressureWashing Business. Retrieved from crazyegg.com/blog/how-to-start-a-pressure-washing-business: Today's Eggspert.

Wikipedia (2022). Pressure Washing. Retrieved from https://en/wikipedia.org.

Watts Steam Store (2022). The Essential Pressure Washer Equipment Start-Up-List. Retrieved from wattssteamstore.com/the-essential-pressure-washer-equipment-start-up-list.